in case of emergency press

We are proud to acknowledge the Traditional Owners of country throughout Australia and to recognise their continuing connection to land, waters, and culture.

We pay our respects to their Elders.

We support recognition, reconciliation, and reparation.

Salt Flats in Heaven

Jack Farrugia

in case of emergency press
https://icoe.com.au
Travancore, Victoria
Australia

Published by in case of emergency press 2024

Copyright © Jack O'Neill 2024
All rights reserved. Without limiting the rights under copyright reserved above, no part of this publication may be reproduced, stored in or introduced into a database and retrieval system or transmitted in any form or any means (electronic, mechanical, photocopying, recording or otherwise) without the prior written permission of both the owner of copyright and the above publishers.

Cover and Title Page photograph: Scott Osborn on Unsplash

ISBN: 978-0-6486111-3-4

This book is dedicated to my brothers

Billy & Tommy

Salt Flats in Heaven

A Play in One Act

by Jack Farrugia

SCENE I

Remote property in the west of New South Wales, Australia. An old Toyota Landcruiser sits in the open beneath a starry night.

HENRY enters with his wounded brother, MICK.

HENRY is in his early thirties. He's physically supporting MICK, mid-thirties, whose thigh is impaled by a star picket.

MICK is clearly in agony, groaning and grimacing, and both men are covered in his blood as they labour toward the Landcruiser.

HENRY helps his brother into the backseat and then looks up to the stars. Awe across his face.

MICK   The fuck you waitin' for? Get her goin'. Go on.

HENRY takes the driver's seat. He starts the Landcruiser on the third attempt and switches on the high-beams.

HENRY   I forgot what the stars were like out here.

MICK grunts.

What the hell were you doing up there so late?

MICK   The beers were tastin' sweet. Nah. I dunno. Time just got away.

HENRY   Well. That's all it does.

MICK   Good spot on a clear night though.

He pauses.

Road's good and straight here. Just watch out for them roos. Pigs too.

HENRY Yeah, I remember. I'm gonna put mum on loudspeaker. She can go see about Judy and the boys.

> *HENRY's eyes stray between his phone and the road. Their mother answers the call.*

MUM [*on phone*] A little late, love, isn't it? What is it?

HENRY It's Mick. Look, don't worry. He's gonna be all right. But we're heading to the hospital. An ambo's gonna meet us halfway. I think...

MUM [*on phone*] Wait. What. What's happened? Michael?

MICK I'm all right, ma.

HENRY He'll be okay. He was up on the cherry picker. He was having a few drinks and, well. He fell. Came down on a rusty star picket. It's gone through his leg and he's losing a lot of...

MUM [*on phone*] Michael? Michael?

MICK Ma, I'm fine. I'm good.

HENRY He's lost some blood. But we're getting help. Listen, mum. I think you should go and be with Judy and the kids. They don't know what's happened. We had to rush off. There wasn't time to go in and tell them. I don't know. Maybe don't wake them. Maybe tell them in the morning when we know more.

MUM [*on phone*] Love. God. Just don't let him pass out. Keep talking to him. Keep him chatty.

HENRY Yeah. That's what they said on the phone.

MICK Ma, it's nothing. Relax.

MUM   [*on phone*] Okay. Keep him up, love. And remember, it's not like driving in the city. Careful of the wildlife. The bastards'll jump.

HENRY   Yep. Mum, you're forgetting I learnt to drive out here. Anyway. I'll call back when we're in the ambo. Gotta focus on the road. Look, mum, he's gonna be fine.

MUM   [*on phone*] I know, love. The angels will take good care of him.

HENRY   Yep. All right. Well, I've gotta…

MUM   [*on phone*] Oh. Hang on, love. Ask Michael if he wants me to irrigate in the morning. Just in case he's gotta stay at the hospital.

HENRY   Mick, mum's…

MICK   Yep. I heard. There's nothin' to irrigate with. We're bone-dry just about. Crop's gone to the dogs anyway.

HENRY   Mum?

MUM   [*on phone*] Yes, love.

HENRY   He said not to worry about it. I'll call once we reach the ambo.

MUM   [*on phone*] Okay, love. Okay. You'll call me then. I'll head down to Mick and Judy's. I'll be up whenever you call.

HENRY   Yep. Talk then.

> *HENRY hangs up. He turns to his brother.*

All right back there?

MICK Fucken paradise, mate.

HENRY All you've gotta do is stay with me, mate. It's all you've gotta do. We'll just talk our way through it. All right?

MICK Well. Yeah. If you're up to it. Swear sometimes I thought you had a muteness or somethin'. When we were kids.

HENRY There was just nobody to talk to out here.

MICK There was us. There was me.

HENRY Maybe. But we've always been a bit too different. It's no secret. We're just wired differently.

MICK You don't know as much as you think you do.

Silence loiters.

HENRY starts humming to the tune of The Little Drummer Boy.

How's Hollywood workin' out for ya?

HENRY Sydney's a long way from Hollywood.

MICK You know what I mean.

HENRY Screenwriting's competitive. I don't know. It's honestly a bit tough at the moment. But it'd be worse if I hadn't got my new prescription. *Much* worse. Those other meds were draining all my creative juices.

MICK Raisin' a crop in a drought's pretty fucken tough too, y'know.

HENRY I bet it is. It's why I'm letting you do it.

MICK   That's good of ya.

HENRY   What's the runt ever gonna offer?

      MICK snorts.

       Dad's words. Not mine.

MICK   Let's not go there, mate. Some other time.

HENRY   Yeah. Yeah, I agree.

MICK   So. Big-shot in the big-smoke. You a big-shot yet?

HENRY   Heard of writer's block? It's like I'm trying to pull the trigger but the gun's freezing up. Like every time. Like I don't know when or where or if I'm gonna find a decent idea.

MICK   Well. What was the last thing you did then?

HENRY   I did some work on a commercial. Some ad for one of those pre-packaged pies. A meat, beef and steak pie. It was for…

MICK   Hold the phone. A *what*?

HENRY   A meat, beef and steak pie.

      MICK recoils in disbelief.

MICK   The fuck are you on about?

HENRY   What do you mean?

MICK   Meat and beef and steak. It's all the same shit, isn't it? That shit's all the same thing.

HENRY   I don't really get what you're trying to say.

MICK   Okay. Well, I dunno. What was actually in the fucken thing?

HENRY There were good chunks of steak in it. Tender strips of beef. A rich mince-meat gravy. All the regular stuff. Pepper. They're quite nice, actually. I've got a freezer full of 'em.

MICK   Christ, mate. Vegan's dream.

HENRY They make a vegan version too.

MICK   What the fuck. Of a beef and meat and steak pie?

HENRY Affirmative. The steak's made of chickpea flour and...

MICK   Yeah. I get it. Anyways. Thought you were into movies, not ads.

HENRY Well, yeah. And in an ideal world my scripts would sell. They'd become actual movies. Movies that people would wanna go and see on a Saturday night.

MICK   So. Must be somethin' in the works. What are ya cookin' up now?

HENRY Nothing. Like I said, I'm going through an ugly case of writer's block. I think it's terminal. This could be the end of me.

> *HENRY turns around and grins, seeking approval for his cheap attempt at humour.*
>
> *MICK gestures for his brother to keep his eyes on the road.*

MICK   Mate. I've got no idea what you actually do. Or if you even do anythin'. None of us do. What've ya actually finished?

HENRY   Plenty of things. My agent threw my last script in the bin, though. I thought it was actually pretty good. I still do.

MICK   What was that one about?

HENRY   You know Gary Oldman? He's a British actor. Been around forever.

MICK   Ah. Fuck. I dunno. What's he in?

HENRY   In films he's played Sid Vicious, Lee Harvey Oswald. Dracula. Churchill. I don't know. He's everywhere. You'd have to know his face.

MICK   Yeah. Well. I don't really have the time for movies, do I.

HENRY clicks his fingers.

HENRY   He was Sirius Black in the Harry Potter franchise.

MICK   Yep, yep. Got ya. He was in the Alcatraz one.

HENRY   What?

MICK   The one where he escapes from Alcatraz.

HENRY   You mean Azkaban?

MICK   [*nodding defensively*] That's what I said.

HENRY   Okay. Whatever. Anyway. So, Gary Oldman plays himself in this story.

MICK   Righto.

HENRY   All right. So, first scene. He's in his swanky home. He's on his laptop in his home office. He's filling out an

	online application form for an Australian visa. A working holiday one. You with me?
MICK	Why the fuck would Gary Oldman do that?
HENRY	Thought you didn't know who he was?

MICK shakes his head, sighs.

MICK	Just get on with it.
HENRY	Okay. Next scene. He's having lunch with his family. He's all perky. He's feasting on his jellied eels and telling them all about how he's gonna pick zucchinis in Bundaberg, learn to surf at Manly. All that stuff.
MICK	You're genuinely an absolute fucken pork chop.
HENRY	You asked so just listen, all right? So. Now it's a week after the family lunch. Gary goes out to the letterbox. There's mail with his name on it. It's from the Australian immigration office. He's wearing this smug grin until he realises they've denied his application. So, there's Gary Oldman. He sinks to his knees in the London rain. He's shaking his fist and he cries, *Curse you, ya bastards! Curse you all!*

Momentary silence.

MICK	That it?
HENRY	Yep. It's only a short film. The best part's the title.
MICK	Well?
HENRY	No Country for Oldman.

HENRY turns around. He's smiling proudly.

MICK	Eyes on the road, ya fucken animal.

HENRY Okay, okay. But do you get the reference in the title?

MICK Look. Mate. I don't. And I don't care to. If that's what you do for a buck then fuck me silly. I sweat my balls off in the field. Every bloody day. While you're dishin' up that rubbish. Now that's a fucken wicked joke. If I say *manual labour* you prob'ly reckon I'm talkin' about some Andalusian bullfighter.

HENRY Okay. Jesus Christ. Don't worry about it.

Silence.

HENRY fiddles with the radio. He can't get it to work.

MICK Wastin' your time, mate. She's buggered.

HENRY Damn. Well. How's your leg now? I can wrap it again if you want. I could use my singlet. Or cut off a leg of my jeans. I don't mind. They were only seven dollars each.

MICK What?

HENRY Huh?

MICK Seven bucks each. What's that mean?

HENRY Oh. Well. I got the *pair* of jeans for fourteen dollars from Vinnies. A pair means two. Half of fourteen is seven.

MICK Yep, all right. *But*. You can only buy them as a pair, ya bloody cretin.

HENRY [*nodding earnestly*] Yeah. Obviously.

MICK buries his head in his hands.

He then momentarily breaks the fourth wall.

SCENE I

MICK   [to the audience] The fuck's wrong with this idiot?

HENRY So, your leg. Do you want it wrapped again?

MICK   Better off not bein' reminded about it. There's some rum in the glovebox. Reckon you could fetch it?

> *HENRY goes rummaging through the glovebox. He picks up a photo and he studies it closely.*

Find it or not?

HENRY Yep. One sec.

> *The photo goes back into the glovebox and HENRY then passes a flask to his brother.*
>
> *MICK drinks.*

MICK   So. Tell me this. Did any of your stories ever get close to bein' a movie ever? Like, y'know, a *real* movie? A proper one.

HENRY Yeah, I guess so. One of them did.

MICK   Well. What was that one about?

HENRY It was about a country music record label in America.

MICK   Like a real one or?

HENRY A fictional one.

MICK   Am I gonna regret askin' about it?

HENRY Do you wanna know or not? Ball's in your court, mate.

MICK   Righto. Whatever. Go on.

HENRY Okay. So, there's this record label called Canned Phish Records.

MICK closes his eyes and shakes his head.

MICK [muttering] Fucksake.

HENRY Anyway, a bunch of artists signed to the record label are nominated for all sorts of awards at this prestigious country music ceremony. Like the biggest one in America. And guess what? They all win. So, it's a good night for Canned Phish Records. And yeah, one by one they go up on stage and accept their awards and they all give speeches in these thick southern accents. They thank god and all that. Including a guy named Bobby Keith Dean. He's the main character. You with me?

No response.

Mick?

HENRY turns around.

MICK's body is gently rocking. He appears unwell.

Mick?

MICK Yeah, mate.

HENRY You look like shit, mate. You okay?

MICK All rosy. Get back to it.

HENRY You sure?

MICK Hundred percent.

HENRY Right. Well. There's an afterparty and we see all the Canned Phish artists enjoying themselves. They're carrying on, they're mingling. Nothing out of the ordinary. But afterwards they have their own private party. So, they're all together. They're out of the public eye. And so all the Canned Phish artists relax. They're all just being themselves. And it turns out none of them are actually American. They've all got strong foreign accents. They're from all over the globe. They were all handpicked by this well-advanced AI program and recruited as young orphans. Mick?

MICK   Yep. Yep. I'm listenin'.

HENRY   Just an example. Bobby Keith Dean's originally from this little Bavarian orphanage. His real name is Hans Schmitz and he's obsessed with the number three. It's obviously the most spiritual of numbers. And that's across many cultures. But he has this burgeoning...

MICK   Mate. Just get on with it.

HENRY   Okay. Right. So. The AI even writes all the songs. Anyway, a flashback reveals that the AI has informed the director of Canned Phish that a certain superstar, our Bobby Keith Dean, or Hans, must die a rockstar death on the night of the awards ceremony as that'll best boost their status, their profile. Their sales will sky-rocket. It's mathematically proven with all the available data. Back in real time, at their private party, everyone is in on the conspiracy. Everyone except Bobby. Obviously. He's got no idea.

MICK   Outdone yourself, haven't ya?

HENRY   At least the colour's back in your voice.

    MICK merely grumbles.

So, the last bit of the story. Bobby's been falling in love with one of the other Canned Phish artists, Polly Jean Lafayette, who's real name is—forget it. Not important. Anyway, Polly's falling in love with him too. It's the first *real* love for both of them. But she ultimately betrays him for the sake of the record label.

MICK drinks, wipes his mouth.

MICK   What the fuck. That was nearly a movie?

HENRY   Nearly. My agent said it was brilliantly crafted. And quite Shakespearean. But he said he wouldn't shop it around since it's not a very original idea. He reckons that everybody suspects that's how the country music industry operates. Everyone's just too afraid to expose the truth for fear of being lynched. Or assassinated. There's some powerful people in that business.

MICK   Are you the full quid?

HENRY   What?

MICK   Fuck it. Forget it.

HENRY   But yeah, the romance is quite nuanced. Quite tragic. And quite profound, actually. That's what my agent said. And he's been around a long time. He knows his shit.

MICK laughs and coughs, coughs and laughs.

What's so amusing?

MICK   The fuck would you know about women?

HENRY   Well. Plenty. I know about love. True love.

MICK   My ass. You seem no different to the gutless weasel you were fifteen years ago. Except now you're content with airin' your dirty laundry to the world.

HENRY   Whatever, mate. I don't really care what you think.

MICK   Righto. Spill the beans then.

> *HENRY clears his throat.*

HENRY   Mick, I'm in love. I have been for a while now.

MICK   Who is she and what's wrong with her? Head like a beaten favourite?

> *He chuckles.*

HENRY   She's the muse of the great Caravaggio. You know, the painter. She might've even been one of his lovers. It's likely. Anyway, I call her Filly.

MICK   Another fella's bird, is she?

HENRY   I don't know what she is now.

MICK   So. What do you's talk about then? Gary Oldman's escape from Alcatraz?

HENRY   Azkaban. It's Az-ka-ban.

MICK   [nodding defensively] That's what I said.

> *HENRY sighs.*

HENRY   Look, with Filly. We don't really talk.

MICK   What do you mean you's don't talk?

HENRY   Well. How do I best put this. She's, ah...

> *HENRY pauses, thumbs his chin.*

MICK [*showing genuine concern*] Sorry, mate. Fuck. She in a coma or somethin'?

HENRY She's dead. Filly's dead. She died in the seventeenth century.

MICK What the...

HENRY She's been dead for hundreds of years. About four hundred.

MICK Cunt, you need a doctor.

HENRY Says the guy with a pole in his leg.

MICK Just fucken drive.

> *Prolonged silence.*
>
> *Until...*
>
> *HENRY farts.*

MICK Frogs are out tonight, aye?

> *No response.*
>
> *Momentary silence.*

Bit crook, mate?

> *MICK winces.*

Wow. Fucken hell. It's really comin' on a bit now. She's comin' on real strong. Somethin' 'specially sinister about it. That's actually atrocious, mate. Fucken disgraceful. Borderline criminal, even.

> *HENRY attempts to stifle his laughter.*
>
> *MICK mock-gags.*

Mate, what the fuck. Put the windows down you fucking animal. Christ. You need professional help. Like immediately. Like a psychologist or somethin'. Pretty agricultural, that is. 'Specially for a bloke who's preferred method of transport is an e-scooter.

The longer MICK rants, the more HENRY laughs. The former seems to enjoy this dynamic.

You realise you actually just soiled my vehicle? Was planning on movin' it on before the financial year's done. Can't be worth two fifths of fuck all now. I can clean the blood out, no problem. But your filth will surely haunt this ute 'til the day I gotta burn it in a field. You got no respect, do ya? You absolute degenerate.

MICK smiles, stretching his arms, then spits out the window.

A hysterical HENRY gradually settles down.

Mate. Seriously though. Fucken hell. That stench was otherworldly.

HENRY   It was probably the ghost of that last meat, beef and steak pie I had.

MICK tilts his head and nods soberly, thoughtfully.

MICK   Yeah. Yeah, I'd say so. That'd likely do it.

SCENE II

> *Middle of nowhere.*
>
> *They're parked by the side of the road. The engine's still running. The headlights are on.*
>
> *MICK's leaning against the front of the Landcruiser, urinating.*
>
> *Further away, HENRY is squatting in the scrub. He's shitting. It's a rather audible affair.*
>
> *Given the distance between them, both men speak in raised voices.*

HENRY   Thought of another one.

MICK   Go on.

HENRY   Cole.

MICK   Cole. Yeah, righto. Cole Beer. That's a genuine fucken beauty.

HENRY   How many's that now?

MICK   Ah, I dunno. A few. Cole Beer. Selma Beer. Phillipa Beer. Nick Beer. Robin Beer. Scott Beer. A reasonably good tally, mate. Done ourselves proud, I reckon.

> *MICK finishes urinating. He painfully struggles to climb into the backseat unassisted.*

HENRY   Hang on, Mick. Stay put. I'll give you a hand when I'm done.

MICK   What about Maia? Maia Beer.

HENRY   Not bad. Oh. Add Noah to the list.

MICK   Noah's all right. What are you gonna use to wipe ya backside?

HENRY   Probably just my sock.

MICK   Judy's left an old Big W catalogue in the backseat here. It's yours if you want it.

HENRY   I'll just use my sock and dump it.

MICK   Righto.

A symphony of HENRY's bowel movements ceases.

HENRY   Daley Beer?

MICK applauds the answer with clapping and whistling.

MICK   Mate. That there's a ripper.

HENRY   Jason?

MICK   Jason Beer. Nah. You're reachin' a bit there. What about Costa?

HENRY   Costa Beer. I'll pay it. Dead serious. I'd actually consider having kids if I had a surname like Beer.

MICK   What if it's like a double surname?

HENRY   What, like a hyphenated one?

MICK   Yeah. That's it. Like that whingin' pommy cricketer. Joe Root-Beer.

HENRY laughs. He farts and he laughs.

HENRY   That's very, very classy work.

MICK   Wait up. Might've just thought of the best one yet.

HENRY   Yeah?

MICK   Yeah. Oliver. Oliver fucken Beer.

> *HENRY falls backward into the scrub. He's tossing about, jeans around his ankles, howling with laughter.*
>
> *He eventually calms himself.*

         You nearly done, mate?

HENRY   Yep. Nearly.

> *Momentary silence while HENRY removes his shoe, then his sock.*

MICK   No way. Henry, you won't fucken believe it. I've just gone and done it, mate. I really believe I just gone and done it. Ya ready for it?

HENRY   You know what, think I just came up with the best...

MICK.   Wait up. Listen. Just listen.

HENRY   [*wiping his arse*] Mick. Mate. You listen. I...

MICK   Strap in, mate. Seatbelts on. My new one'll blow your fucken hair back.

HENRY   Just hear me out. I think I have...

MICK   Tobias Beer.

SCENE III

> *The brothers are back on the road.*
>
> *They're snacking on dried apricots, passing the bag back and forth between them.*
>
> *The bag now arrives in HENRY's possession.*

MICK   [chewing a mouthful] Righto. I'm good. Put 'em away before you shit yourself again.

> *HENRY obliges. He places the bag in the glovebox, from which he again takes the photo.*
>
> *He glances at the photo, then passes it back to his brother.*
>
> *MICK smiles. With glassy eyes he looks over the photo before sliding it into his breast pocket.*

HENRY   Your boys are getting big.

MICK   Time will do that to 'em.

> *MICK yawns. He swigs from the flask.*

HENRY   How old's Pat now?

MICK   Seven. Eight, nearly.

HENRY   He's got your nose.

MICK   Poor bastard.

> *They casually share a laugh.*

They're the best kids, mate. The best kids.

HENRY   [nodding] Yeah, I know.

MICK No. You don't. You really don't. You were never 'round to see 'em grow up.

HENRY I was never gonna come back with dad still around.

MICK You had plenty of chances since.

HENRY pinches the bridge of his nose. He rubs his eyes.

MICK Anyhow. I'm not gonna be like the old man. I won't get on my boys' asses about farmin'. Not a chance, mate. I want 'em to go and do their thing like you gone and done. Unless all they wanna do is raise crop. But I'd doubt it.

HENRY I'm sure they'll make the right calls when they have to.

MICK scoffs.

MICK You're sure, are ya? You don't even know 'em, mate.

HENRY Okay. I get it. You're right. But be honest. Have you ever wanted out?

MICK Well. Can't leave now, can I? Too set in my ways. And I don't much wanna stay. Just the way it goes.

HENRY Between a rock and a hard place.

MICK Yep. Between a rock and a hard place. Or maybe it's the opposite, y'know? Fuck. I dunno what I'm sayin' now. It's just like I got lost or somethin'. Look, forget it. Where the fuck's this fucken ambo?

HENRY You can try explaining it, mate. If you want to.

MICK Henry. Mate. What if I *can't*?

HENRY You can try. It's your call.

> *MICK sighs mournfully.*

MICK   Maybe it's like bein' a passenger in your own car.

> *He knocks a fist on his forehead. He opens the fist before his eyes. Examines his hand. Watches how it trembles.*

Well. Nah. Maybe it's like this. You know the way your tongue knows its way 'round your mouth? Like it knows all the contours on the roof of your mouth. It knows that gap where ya had a molar pulled. Knows it well. And that flat tip of a fang 'cause your grindin' ya teeth to dust every bloody night. Yeah, your tongue knows it's terrain. It ain't ever lost, is it? Not even in the dark. Not unless you cut it out. Well, I dunno what's gone on. But I'm feelin' more and more like the tongue that's got cut out.

> *He laughs nervously. Coughs.*

HENRY   Mick. What's going on, mate?

MICK   Just lost my bearings is all. Ain't a big deal, mate.

HENRY   What's Judy say about it?

MICK   Well. She doesn't know, does she? And she's never gonna. This shit stays between us.

HENRY   There's ways to get help.

> *No response.*
>
> *A moment later and HENRY colours in the silence by whistling to the tune of* The Little Drummer Boy.
>
> *He stops abruptly.*

Mahatma.

MICK   What?

HENRY   Mahatma Beer. Not bad, right?

> *MICK's laughing morphs into an ugly fit of coughing.*

HENRY   Ambo can't be far, mate. You're gonna hang on.

MICK   Righto, boss.

HENRY   Ask me something. Anything. I don't care.

> *MICK scratches his stubble as he ponders.*

MICK   Righto. Well. Here's one. What's hell, ya reckon?

HENRY   I don't know. I don't know if I believe in that sort of stuff. Well, not really. I don't know, mate.

MICK   Nah. Me neither.

HENRY   Go ahead. Ask something else. I'm not shy, mate.

MICK   Yeah, nah. You really aren't. Fucken learnt that the hard way.

HENRY   [tapping the dashboard] Another question. Shoot.

MICK   It's okay, mate. I just want the silence.

> *MICK's breathing heavily now.*
>
> *HENRY orientates the rear-vision mirror to focus on his brother.*

HENRY   Look, Mick. The ambo's gotta be close. I just need to know you're with me until then.

MICK   I'm good.

HENRY   You sound like shit. You look like shit.

MICK   Me or your movie career?

> *MICK laughs and wheezes, wheezes and coughs.*

HENRY   Mick, mate. I'm not in the mood. I'm fucking stressed. All right? My first night back wasn't supposed to go like this. Like I said, just let me know you're here with me.

MICK   All right, mate. Goin' nowhere.

> *HENRY nods stoically.*

Why don't ya tell me about that bird you fancy.

HENRY   Filly?

MICK   Yeah. Filly. It's a good name, that.

HENRY   Well. I don't know. I know she was famous for her beauty. And I know she died fairly young. And obviously she modelled for Caravaggio a bunch of times. She's in a handful of his paintings that still exist. I wouldn't know a thing about her otherwise.

MICK   Where's the bloke now?

HENRY   Are you kidding?

MICK   Course, mate. Cunt's been dead about four hundred years, I reckon. Well. That's if my maths holds up.

> *HENRY, seemingly surprised that his brother had been listening, turns around and smiles.*

Eyes on the road, little brother.

> *Momentary silence.*

So tell me this, then. How do ya know it's love? You never even seen her properly.

HENRY   Well. I did, actually. I did see her once.

MICK   [*rolling his eyes*] Fuck. Here we go.

HENRY   Look. Don't worry about it.

MICK   Just pullin' ya leg, mate. Go on. I wanna hear about it.

HENRY looks at his brother in the rear-vision mirror and nods.

HENRY   Okay. So, way back she modelled for a portrait of Saint Catherine. It's unreal. *She's* unreal. It's in an art gallery in Madrid nowadays. I used to search it online whenever I was...

MICK   Mate. Stop. Don't finish that sentence. Just in case.

HENRY   Fuck off. Anyway, I'd been wanting to see the painting up close for the longest time. You know, to be in the same room as it. To be near enough to *touch* it. So. A few years back when I was in Europe I took an expensive detour to Madrid to go and see it. And guess what? Yep. It'd been pulled from the wall that very morning to undergo some restoration work. Just the worst timing. And it wasn't like I could wait it out in Madrid for ten days. I was almost broke. Anyway, I was due to fly home from Dublin the following night.

MICK   So. You're fucked, are ya?

HENRY   Yeah. Pretty fucked.

MICK   Did you see her or not?

HENRY turns around and flashes a grin.

HENRY   I check my wallet. I've got forty euros in cash. So, a hushed bribe and forty euros later and I'm being led

	out the back by this rough Spanish guy. A guy who works there.
MICK	[*clapping*] Cheeky bugger.
HENRY	And yeah. So there she is, my Filly. Alone. Leaning against a wall. Just the most divine thing you'll ever see.
MICK	Good for you, mate.

He drinks.

HENRY	There's more.
MICK	Yeah?
HENRY	Yep. So. I must've only been with her for two or three minutes before the Spaniard throws me out. Which was bullshit. We'd agreed on ten minutes. So, I tried…
MICK	[*leaning forward*] Should've flogged the bastard.
HENRY	He looked like a prime Gordon Tallis. Same murderous eyes and everything.
MICK	[*leaning back*] Righto. Play on.
HENRY	So, out I go. It hits me that I may never see Filly again. Hits me like a fucking freight train. I don't know. I was pretty dejected. Anyway, I go walking through the city. I'm aimlessly walking around for hours. And then I get tired of walking and tired of all the crowds and all I wanna do is just be alone.

He pauses. He exhales in a pronounced fashion.

So, I walk into this random church. It's dead quiet in there. There's just me and a group of monks doing their monk things. They're scattered all around the pews. They're on their knees with their heads bowed and they're praying, I suppose. So, I take the stairs at the back to this little loft where it's just me. Me and my view of the church below. The monks doing their monk things. And there's this peculiar scent of...

MICK   Get on with it.

He drinks.

HENRY   Right. So, get this. Hung high above the altar is this life-sized timber cross with Jesus on it. It's pretty standard. You know, it's the cross. It's Jesus. It's his body. His ribs, his wounds. But. But. The head. The face. It's Filly's. It's hers. It's her just as she appears in the painting of Saint Catherine. It sounds insane, I know. But I swear that's exactly what happened. Look. I know you won't believe me but it wasn't just a face carved of wood. I can't really explain it. It was *alive*. Her eyes were alive. Her whole face was. You must think I'm nuts. But I swear it. Mick, I swear I...

MICK taps HENRY on the shoulder and hands him the flask.

MICK   Henry, mate. There's only a bit left. You should finish it.

HENRY reluctantly takes the flask. He drains what remains of the rum in two gulps. He cringes, burps.

I mean this, mate. I believe ya. I really do. I'm not takin' the piss. Just wanted you to know that.

HENRY   Yeah. Right. I know you think it's a load of shit.

MICK   So. What happened next?

HENRY   [*shaking his head*] Forget it.

MICK   I seen shit too, y'know. Shit I can't explain. Demons. Angels. I never told anybody that before.

> *HENRY turns around and for a moment the brothers gravely lock eyes.*
>
> *They nod in turn.*
>
> *Eyes back on the road.*

        So, what happened?

HENRY   She spoke to me.

MICK   What'd she say?

HENRY   She said, *Come to me. Fly to me.* That's exactly what she said. And so I call out to her. I'm asking her to show me how. I'm begging her. I'm begging her to give me wings. It was all so bizarre. It was so confusing. But—but so heavenly.

MICK   I believe ya, mate. How'd it resolve?

HENRY   I must have been causing a scene, I guess. One minute it's just me and Filly. And then suddenly I'm getting handled by the monk guys. I'm kicking and screaming as they drag me down the stairs, as they throw me outside. A few of them pin me down. Eventually a couple of cops come by and take me away. Back to my hotel. And that was that. I flew to Dublin early the next morning. Then got on my way back to Sydney.

> *Silence.*

        Mick? Mick?

MICK   [*grumbling*] Here, mate.

> *MICK's condition is rapidly worsening.*

HENRY   You need to hang on, mate. The ambo really can't be far off now.

MICK   Hang on? *Hang on?* All I do is hang on. You got no idea how tough shit gets out here.

HENRY   I obviously do. Otherwise I'd never have left. Mate, it's far too hot. It's too boring, too lonely. The work is too hard. It's my idea of hell. I only came back because I thought a week in hell might inspire my writing. I tried just about everything else.

MICK   [*barely audible as he's struggling to keep his eyes open*] It wasn't a fall. I jumped.

HENRY   What's that, mate? You're gonna have to speak up.

MICK   It's nothin'.

> *The Landcruiser jolts and skids.*
>
> *When it comes to a halt, HENRY gets out to inspect for damage.*

HENRY   [*privately*] Fucking tyre's blown.

> *He returns to the cabin to switch on the hazard lights.*

There's a busted tyre I've gotta change. I'll go as fast as I can, okay?

MICK   [*groggily*] Right.

HENRY   Hang tight, mate.

> *HENRY gathers the wrench and the jack and the spare tyre and goes about removing the busted one.*

[raised voice] Well. I told you about what I think hell is. Wanna hear about my idea of heaven?

Silence.

[raised voice] Mick?

HENRY suspends the task at hand to check on his brother.

Mick?

MICK responds with a fragile smile and a thumbs-up.

HENRY nods, then resumes changing the tyre.

[raised voice] Okay. Well. There's these salt flats out in Utah. In America. I saw a doco on them years ago. Maybe seven or eight years ago now. And that landscape's just never left my mind. I think it's the most breathtaking place on earth. So, that's where my heaven is. And in my heaven there's this permanent sunset. All these impossibly beautiful colours. Soft pastel colours mixed in with the electric ones. And the colours are all changing like they do at sunset. They're changing but the sky never goes dark.

He pauses as he rolls away the old tyre, starts fitting the new one.

[raised voice] And there's nobody around but me and Filly. It's just us. We're cruising around on a motorcycle with her on the back. She's holding me so tightly, so warmly. And here and there are all these stacks of Styrofoam boxes. You know, like a stack you'd see on a pallet in some warehouse or something. Anyway, so there's dozens and dozens of these stacks. And all we're doing is cruising around. And when we wanna, we go crashing through a stack of boxes. We come out the other side buzzing. Laughing. And feeling so fucking carefree. We know we're dead but we feel so alive. And then we go through another stack. And another. It's just so perfect, mate. I can't really do it justice in words. But that's my idea of heaven. What do you reckon? Mick?

> *Silence.*
>
> *Then, when HENRY rises to check on his brother, sirens can be heard. Faintly whirling at first. Then rising, nearing.*
>
> *Distant lights flashing. Red and blue.*
>
> *HENRY staggers toward the advancing ambulance. One hand guards his eyes, the other he waves frantically overhead.*

[yelling] Hear that, Mick? They're coming. It's the angels. They're on their way.

> *He turns back to the Landcruiser, the hazard lights still flashing.*

[yelling] They're on their way, mate. The angels are coming. Do you hear the angels, Mick? Mick?

> *HENRY flinches as a kangaroo suddenly skips past. He watches the kangaroo until it bounds away into the darkness and is gone from sight.*
>
> *He then admires the stars before again setting his eyes on the Landcruiser.*

[yelling] Mick, mate. It's the angels. Mick?

CURTAIN

About the Author

Photograph of author: Erin Comensoli

Born in 1994, Jack Farrugia is a Maltese-Australian poet and playwright.

Salt Flats in Heaven is his first play.

In 2023, he published The Tercets, available from **in case of emergency press**.

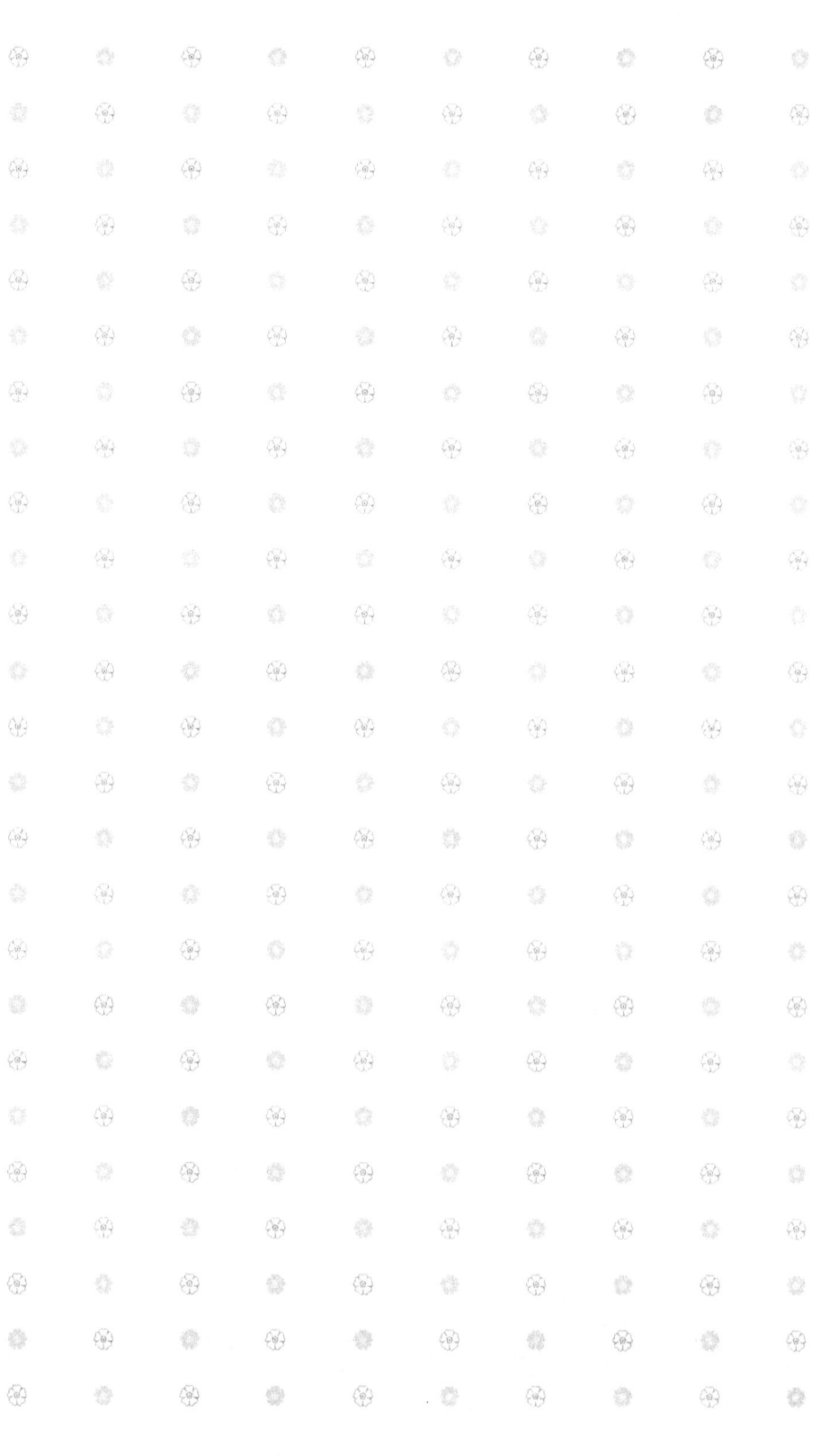

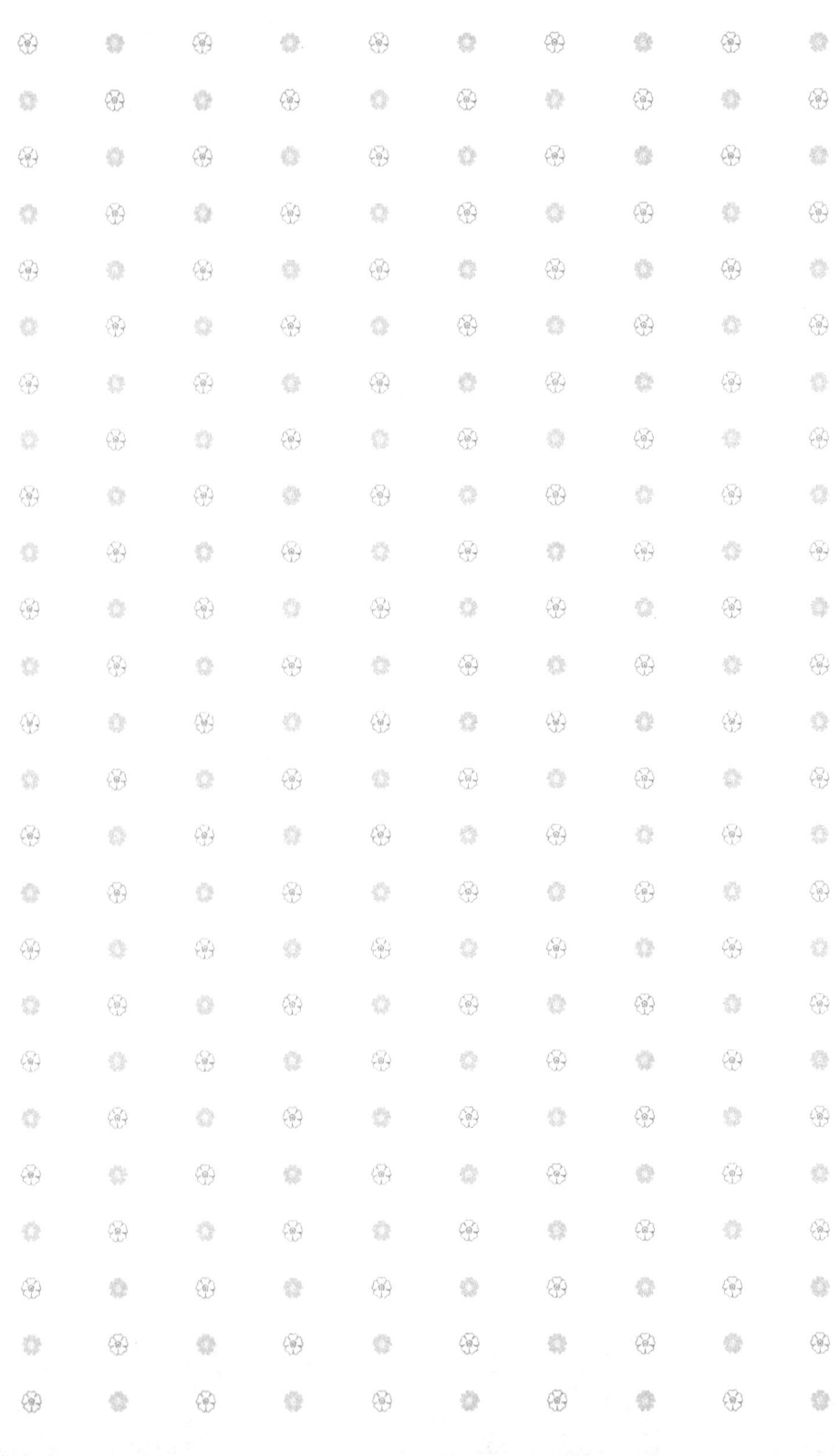

www.ingramcontent.com/pod-product-compliance
Lightning Source LLC
Chambersburg PA
CBHW022022290426
44109CB00015B/1281